# Second Looks

## Memoir in Essay and Poetry

# Second Looks

Memoir in Essay and Poetry

Mary L. Gardner

Clare Songbirds Publishing House Poetry Series
ISBN  978-1-957221-36-6
Clare Songbirds Publishing House
*Second Looks* © 2026 Mary L. Gardner



Printed in the United States of America
FIRST EDITION

140 Cottage Street
Auburn, New York  13021
www.claresongbirdspub.com

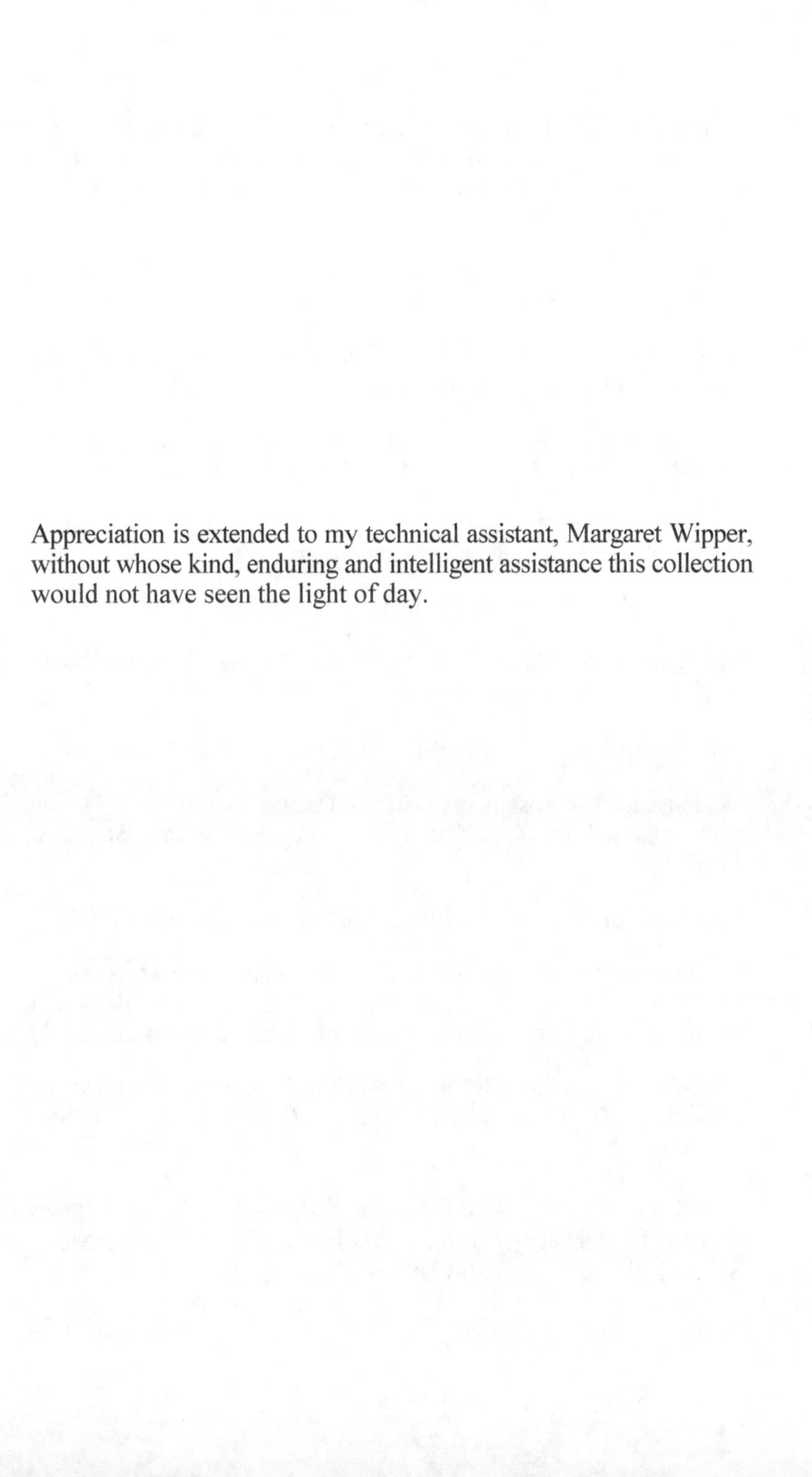

Appreciation is extended to my technical assistant, Margaret Wipper, without whose kind, enduring and intelligent assistance this collection would not have seen the light of day.

# Acknowledgements

Grateful acknowledgment is made to editors of the following publications and coordinators of competitive calls for poetry or essay in which pieces from this collection have been selected for inclusion or awards.

"On the Issue of Provenance" & "Between Times" - Clare Songbirds Publishing House, *Elizabeth Royal Patton Poetry Prize Anthology* (2024)

"Egg, " "Bouquet," & "A Place of Her Own" - FootHills Publishing, *When All Danger of Frost is Past*, (2015)

*Peaches* - National League of American Pen Women, Inc. (NLAPW), *Grace K. Wofford Award*, 2nd Place (2022)

"A Tradition in Danger of Disappearing" - Upstate Medical University, *The Healing Muse Anthology* (2023)

"Field Study" - FootHills Publishing, *Place Settings* (2017)

"Self Talk, A New Place" - NLAPW, The PenWoman, *Stanislavsky's Student, after E.Hopper, Automat 1927* (Winter 2010)

"Struggling Haiku" - NLAPW, *The Penwoman* (2008)

"Moonscape" - Rosamond Gifford Lecture Series, *W.S.Merwin Competition*, First Place (2010) Published in *The Post-Standard,* 11/08/10

*Why Funerals Matter* - 1st Place, *The Skaneateles Press* (2005)

"Woman in the Window" - NLAPW, The Penwoman Press, *Happy Birthday Mr. Lincoln: Commemorative Collage*. Published in invitation from The U.S.Lincoln Bicentennial Commission (2009)

"Solo" - Cayuga Lake Books, *From the Finger Lakes: A Memoir Anthology* (2021) & *NLAPW Marion Doyle Award*, 3rd Place (2024)

"Last Conversation" - NLAPW, *The Pen Woman, Della Crowder Award*, First Place (Summer 2014) and *Art & Poetry Show*, Second Place, The Tech Garden, Syracuse (2013)

"Gift of Unknowing"- FootHills Publishing, *Place Settings* (2017)

I am grateful to family, friends and colleagues who have encouraged me for years, and who have, from time to time, read some pieces and offered their comments.

For as much as I can remember – I am always seeking accuracy and insight in my work and hope that effort is confirmed here. I am grateful to all those of humankind, especially, but also, to other inhabitants of nature here and there, who have inspired me and gifted me with enduring memories and stories.

# Contents

## About *Second Looks*

One blessing of having lived a long life is to have accumulated stories and snippets of stories that, with memory-work and reflection, can become the stuff of "memoir." Whatever the proper name, stories and story-telling are revered art forms in all cultures. Perry Ground, Storyteller, Haudenosaunee Confederacy, writes in *American Indian*, National Museum of the American Indian, Summer 2024: "The cultural information, the historical information, the beliefs, the values, just the life stories that exist within the stories are really part of what makes us human beings."

*Second Looks* is just that – a collection of stories told in essay and poetry which have emerged at different times in my life. Some have been published, others I have ignored until now. It's like literary hindsight. Anais Nin writes in defense of this retrospective approach: "There are very few human beings who receive the truth, complete and staggering, by instant illumination. Most of us acquire it fragment by fragment, on a small scale, by successive developments, cellularly like a laborious mosaic." In this collection, each essay is followed by one or more poems which bear some connection to the essay, and sometimes, to other essays. Rarely, did I write a particular essay and poem at the same time. The subject matter is not always autobiographical except in how I tell the story. I was not in Indonesia in December 2004 when the Great Tsunami devastated that part of the world., but I was consumed by the news accounts. I imagined myself at the national memorial celebration of Rosa Park's life on October 25, 2005, when her body lay in state in the U.S. Capitol. It was easy to place myself as the lone young woman in Edward Hopper's painting, "Automat 27" – hearing, seeing, feeling whatever might have been her story – and leaving those thoughts in the poem, "Bouquet." As recently as yesterday, it remains a pleasure to remember being in the presence of Queen Anne Lace on a country road, day after day, walking back and forth to our one-room country school for seven years and seeing masses of these endearing wildflowers standing tall in fields and among roadside rubble where I was walking. Sometimes, I and my companions – typically, my sisters – would just stop and run our fingers over the blossoms.

Finally, as the "Evelyn's Gift" essay in this collection unfolded, I became keenly aware of the gifts I have received through all these stories – essay and poetry – that are either described or implied throughout this manuscript. I invite you to read on, to let your stories come to mind between the lines I've laid down here and take another look at your own.

# On the Issue of Provenance

Have you considered the provenance of a poem—
how it came to be, what inspired its unfolding
across the page, when its journey is complete?

Is a poem not nurtured in invention summoned
from what we have lived or mused upon or left
in the barely conscious? Or learned and applied
from the work of noted poets, past and present?

And does not the discovery itself enliven
the quest, whatever the choices one employs
in the poem's subsequent telling?

As one given to unfettered reads and re-writes,
first to myself and later with colleagues,
am I not thus gifted with new insights and options,
perhaps a re-visioning of the truth I seek to tell?

Having given these questions due consideration,
and certainty being a matter of choice,
I cannot say a poem is mine
except to own the effort.

# Of Coops and Eggs
*"Inflation and avian flu have driven up the  price of eggs,"*
*New York Times, 2/3/2023*


An egg. Humble, everyday thing. In recent times, the topic of "eggs"—their high cost and scarcity – has occupied a prominent space in news outlets across America, the likely culprits being inflation and price gouging, fuel prices up and down, a diminishing work force, and lagging supply chain for this important agricultural business. And lurking like a curse, the deadly Avian flu. Eggs are critical to our way of life, served for breakfast or lunch or dinner. Think cafes, confectionaries, holiday feasts. Americans are said to eat 278 of them a year (NY Times, 2/3/23). This morning, I opened my refrigerator to find I am down to two eggs which I will either sauté for myself or save for a recipe requiring the same.

Who knew. Until two months ago, I purchased two dozen eggs every two weeks from my professional farmer friend, who treats her thirty-member flock and their insulated coop with utmost care. Until trauma caused by a hungry fox, she allowed her flock free roam of yard and field or kept them in a moveable fenced "pasture." Due to deadly fighting in her flock, occasional disease outbreaks, and current production costs, she is maintaining her flock for personal use only. She tells me egg cartons labeled in some variation of "raised on vegetarian diet" do no favor to the hens and their resident roosters. Chickens are omnivores, she says. Set them to roam freely on grass or field and watch them scratch and dig for bugs and worms, as well as weeds, grass, even tiny stones.  Some ambitious and frustrated people are buying chicks to raise in their back yards and harvest their own eggs. I predict this idea will be short-lived except among all but the very determined.

Raising chickens is hard work and expensive. I should know. I grew up with chickens – enjoying fresh eggs and fried or baked chicken for Sunday dinners. My mother, father, three sisters, and I lived in the house where my mother and her father were born and grew up. Our twenty-six- acre farm included a barn, car garage, roadside stand where my grandparents had sold farm goods, and a chicken coop in the backyard down near the creek. I remember cleaning the coop, watching for signs of a preying fox, keeping the henhouse at acceptable temperatures throughout the year, and tolerating free-range chickens in yard and garden. The land was a mix of untilled fields, a small garden, a narrow stream that flooded its banks occasionally, a once-productive apple orchard, and a stand of box elder trees which grew wild and provided timber for our Tuscarora neighbors who crafted the wood into domestic and artistic objects.

Every two or three years, the roadside stand took on another role, becoming a perfect place for growing our poultry and eggs business. We would purchase a small flock of chicks—tiny fluffy yellow birds that moved around continuously in a light-heated "brooder." My father surrounded the brooder with a construction of box and fine mesh fencing. We enjoyed watching them grow, day to day, occasionally holding them, losing them, capturing them and returning them to the brooder. When they reached pullet size, we slowly introduced them to roaming the yard, not going near the road, staying out of the garden, not messing around with my mother's flowers, and adjusting to coop life down by the creek. I remember two or three summers when we had more young chickens than we needed. That occasioned preparing them for sale to a few egg customers who were delighted to purchase them, slaughtered and delivered to their doors. I hated this ugly task despite recognizing that someone had to do it. Even now, this part of the story can come to mind when I purchase commercially wrapped chicken— whole or in parts—and give a nod to the folks who are assigned to these jobs on some conveyor belt in a walled-in, roofed over, maybe temperature-controlled, building. We pared down the flock to zero as my sisters and I gradually left home for college. The coop remained but served no further use. It was simply part of the "property for sale" when my parents relocated to live near their daughters with families of their own and no barns or coops.

Now, I am accustomed to purchasing cartons of eggs, preferably organic—brown or white—and storing them in the refrigerator. I remain firmly of the opinion, that when it comes to eggs, there is nothing like an egg gifted by a chicken housed in a clean coop and roost, allowed free range on pasture or grass, and, perhaps, on speaking terms with its caretaker.

## An Egg, A Cup

There's something compelling about a soft-cooked egg
Served warm, upright, resting in a stemmed cup.

Tap it lightly with a knife where it slopes
To oval.  Lift off its lid.  Inside, a surprise! Behold

Its barely set world of yolk and white, complete unto itself.
Slide your spoon around the edge, through swirling

Lines of gold and take a spoonful to your tongue.
A taste so grand – the humble egg served warm,
Upright, resting in a stemmed cup. Virtue unsung.

# Peaches

*"...When I bring sweet things to your greedy hands I know*
*why there is honey in the cup of the flowers and why fruits are secretly*
*filled with sweet juice..."*
*Rabindranath Tagore (1861-1941)*


Tagore had it right more than one hundred years ago. Back in the days when I was a concert singer, I sometimes included J.A. Carpenter's song setting of this poem. I remember having a salivary response to the fruit-filled-with-sweet-juice line. I could taste Peaches every time I sang the song, feel the juices on my chin, my hands. I've come to see why speaking it aloud—"sweet things… greedy hands…honey in the cup…" remains a pleasure. Peaches were a prominent item in my family—eating and canning them, serving them to guests. We had lots of company, especially on Sundays, sometimes for dinner which might include fresh corn on the cob, as well. Often, guests arrived without notice, so we planned for them on Saturdays. Peaches on cake or ice cream was a favorite dessert choice for these and other occasions.

Every August, my parents scoured local farms to find the best of the harvest. Upon bringing the peaches home, my mother, three sisters and I set to work, canning at least two bushels. It was a group thing, an organized process, tasked sequentially though we could change work stations midway: rinsing, peeling and pitting, ladling them into a hot water bath for three minutes, and dropping them into waiting sterile jars. Alternating work stations was important and diplomatic on my mother's part, since we girls could be clumsy or slow, especially at peeling and pitting, whether by design or failed effort. There was little patience for resistance or argument. Mother insisted on three-quarters cup of sugar added to each jar, to be stirred gently down the sides with a knife, taking care not to puncture the fruit. We sealed and placed them—seven jars at a time – into a canner rack in hot water, bringing the water to a boil and cooking them for twenty minutes. We lifted out the heavy rack and set it on a counter to cool. Next morning, we laid the jars carefully on their sides, leaving them there until the sugar disappeared into the fruit. I remember Mother laying clean dishtowels over them, pausing, putting her hands on her hips, and saying to no one in particular something like, "There. Done. I think they are perfect!" Often, she would then pick up our old party phone and call a friend to report our success.

Twenty-plus years ago, my husband and I were living in our historic home some three hundred miles away from my parents. I was approaching a marker birthday and feeling nostalgic for my family and favored childhood days and routines. I was also looking for new ideas for entertaining friends. I thought about Peaches. I approached two friends and asked them to join me in canning a bushel or two and we would share the results. They declined nicely, saying what I already feared might be their response. We have ready access to Peaches in season, fresh from markets and fields, sometimes straight from basket to mouth leaving little time to taste slow salivary prompts to memory. Further, grocery stores are well stocked with Peaches. Think Dole.

So, I took on confidence and desire, and began the process alone. Mother wrote me some directions, saying of the last step (laying the filled jars on their sides), "In a few words, any time you go by them, give them a turn…your porch would be a good location. When you are sure they are cold, loosen the seal rings and you will hear them make a sound like a bell. That's a sign they are done." I drew a sense of peace from walking by the jars resting quietly on my porch. Turning them over was like caring for them and part of the contract for their ultimate gift in return. Mother's letter is a treasured page in my kitchen library. I am always amazed at her perfect handwriting, even though she could not go beyond the second year of high school because of her widowed mother's need for care. Her handwriting still evokes her voice for me, though I must confess I never heard the bell ring.

One Sunday evening the following winter, we had guests unexpectedly for a light supper. I knew just what would be perfect for dessert…Peaches. I went to the basement, opened a jar and let the Peaches rest a while on the counter. I topped each small bowl of ice cream with two Peach halves and a little chocolate sauce, and served them with the attention they deserved. Our guests were likewise pleased with the presentation and taste, perhaps the novelty of the story.

I never again tried canning Peaches alone. It's a group thing. I've tried freezing them for the long days of winter and they're good. But not the same at all.

## A Tradition in Danger of Disappearing

*Inspired by illustrated message on table napkin:*
*"Enjoy the small moments"*


Last week, I was a guest at a morning "Coffee,"
offered with grace and simplicity.

> *Hot Cross Buns, apples quartered,*
> *Coffee, tea, cups and saucers,*
> *Napkins folded on small plates,*
> *Bowl of early tulips, six chairs.*

Invitations had been extended and welcomed
despite short notice and light snow overnight—
not issues for those of a certain age who know
that gatherings of similar dimension delighted

generations past as they can in the present,
who embrace a mindset bending toward
living well, living long, living with joy
wherever good fortune sets them down.

It remains for us to pass it on—
to make time for small moments, perhaps
stolen out of hurried lives, not ruled by
style or space or time or notice given.

## Field Study

*If I had stood at the edge of the field, quiet and attentive,*
    would I have seen them growing tall
    somewhere between my knees and an elephant's eye
    or heard the rustle of their husks at dusk
    after a long hot day in the sun?

*Would I have guessed the towering tassel's role,*
    sending pollen on the wind midway down the stalk
    to one lone shank, there
    to kiss the flowering silks,
    each to birth one kernel?

*Would I have noticed the close-knit planting of rows*
    side by side, holding strong against wind and rain?
    Or would I have thought it merely a ploy
    to confuse a scampering field mouse
    or a child running a maze in late September?

*Their season spent now, they lie bent and triangled into furrows,*
*turning to gold and brown, giving back as they have taken,*
*leaving me to nod in their direction some notion of thanks*
    for their sweet plump fruit
      served up on a summer afternoon
    to the delight of discriminating palates
    and poets pondering the wonder of these things.

# Power in a Pot of Tea

In September 1959, I moved into a beautiful old mansion on East Avenue in Rochester N.Y. St. Elizabeth Guild House had been converted into a residence for "young working ladies." Just as it is today, East Avenue was a main thoroughfare from towns and villages along the New York State Thruway into the city, home of Eastman Kodak, Xerox, University of Rochester, Eastman School of Music, and other notable names. Like the grand old homes and sturdy brick apartment buildings along this corridor of Rochester's former glory days, the Guild House was set back from the street by a broad lawn and well-maintained old trees.

I had just graduated from nearby Nazareth College, having earned a baccalaureate degree in sociology and a minor in speech and drama. I had lived off campus and worked many part-time jobs. My parents wanted me to return home after graduation, find a job, marry and settle down. I had other ideas. While I cherished our home where my grandfather was born – the orchard, woods and garden, treasured memories of walking to country school and masses of wild flowers along the road—I also knew I had to plant my dreams in other soil, that this transition to professional employment and independent living could mean huge opportunities to grow personally, socially and culturally without the boundaries set by family. Both excited and nervous about what lay ahead, I took a program director position at the Charles Settlement House, a social agency and community center serving largely Italian and German families and a growing population of recently immigrated Puerto Rican families and individuals.

The Guild House became my residential community for that first year after graduation. It was safe and affordable. I paid twenty -two dollars weekly for room and board, which meant breakfast and dinner daily and a single room and shared bath in a first floor four-room wing of the house. Three of us were employed full time in the city and were in early stages of establishing our professional careers. The fourth person was employed in a part-time job which I don't recall. She suffered a significant stutter and anxiety and was fairly self-isolated. I don't remember how this began, but one evening she asked me to help her deal with the stutter issue. Perhaps I had told her that I was active in singing groups in college and maybe singing would help. In any event, we worked together over a few weeks on this problem, singing a cappella in our wing of the house when no one else was around. She improved a little and we agreed to take a break. I did not have contact with her after I moved out one year later.

Dinner at the Guild House was served in the dining room around a table which seated the whole house—about twenty of us, of whom a dozen or so were young women in their late teens or early twenties. Dinner was served family style, with platters beginning randomly at one end of the table or the other. I soon recognized that the platters were empty as they neared the opposite end of the table, causing obvious stress and conflict. I decided to use my leverage as a newly minted social worker to investigate the empty platters. (I had just learned that St. Elizabeth's Guild House was itself a social agency: one third of the residents were wards of the court and two thirds were employed young women who were expected to exercise some discrete positive influence just by living there.) It turned out that some kitchen workers were taking what should have been served to us. The situation was remedied and I was not identified.

We poured our coffee from large thermos urns. Hot tea could be requested and was served in individual teapots with teabags hung inside. These were carried in by staff and offered to us individually. I noticed that hot tea was becoming an increasingly popular choice among the younger residents. When I asked about this, one resident explained, "I like having a teapot all to myself. All the water. My own teabag. No sharing anything."

I learned a lot that year, just spending time in our shared living areas or waiting to use the ironing board in the lower-level laundry room. Younger residents liked to hang out there, smoke cigarettes, talk among themselves. They had already lived through some tough times, many having come through the foster care and/or juvenile justice systems. Some had failed in academic or employment settings. Some, perhaps many, had suffered through some form of abuse, but that subject drew only casual mention, as though it was a common experience. My life issues – income, career, friends, missing my family, exploring my inner self – paled by comparison. They seemed to feel safe enough to be candid about themselves with me, and perhaps with other older residents of the house. I never asked. I found myself being more attentive and transparent in response to their queries about my life – family, schooling, work experience, etc. My having spent seven years in a one-room school drew questions and laughs, like something quaint, peculiar for sure. While I was candid in response, I was always aware of maintaining the social distance expected of me. They insisted on absolute honesty and fairness about everything. They could be funny and smart, especially about what they saw as "uppity" behaviors among themselves or others. Tempers could flare in a minute, often interrupted by one of them or by the mere calming presence of us older residents moving through our shared areas.

Another resident and I developed a friendship over conversations at mealtimes, meeting up in the lounge, and occasionally going to movies or one of the few restaurants nearby. She was secretary for one of Xerox's top executives, a small growing company that went public two or three years later. While born into a local immigrant Polish family, she wanted to move out and live independently. As we came to recognize our similar goals, we decided to try living together; we left St. Elizabeth's together in 1960 and rented an apartment nearby. We lived there for three years before moving on separately.

Now, sixty years later, I see how this experience at St. Elizabeth's Guild House fits in my life journey. Today, we might call it a "group home." I never researched how "Guild" got into that name. I am especially aware of what I learned from the younger residents: lifestyles can be knit together and built out of very little; a strong ego can prevail in the most trying situations; compassion and fairness can almost always save the day; respect is the core of mutually enriching relationships regardless of social class. If I could, I would thank them. Maybe that's what happened a few years ago, when, occasionally, a young woman and I exchanged smiles and brief greetings on Montgomery Street in Syracuse when I was on my way to class at the Downtown Writers Center and she was exiting St. Paul's food and hospitality center. Now, that I think about it, I hope she favors a little pot of tea. Just for herself.

# Her Life's Work and Mine

I took out her picture today, looked at it closely, held it in my lap. Aunt Agnes, aka Sister Mary Leonard, OP, my father's sister. She was my favorite relative, beyond my parents and sisters. Given the constraints of my downsized home, I keep the photo in a box with other collectibles. It's a very good close-up portrait, 1940's vintage, professionally matted and framed. She is seated next to the piano, reading to two small children, a girl and boy. Dressed in the traditional Dominican sister's garb in black and off-white, the camera caught her in a typical setting when she was a beloved and much heralded kindergarten teacher.

A member of the Dominican Sisters of Grand Rapids, Michigan, Aunt Agnes earned her master's degree at Notre Dame University in the 1940's, a remarkable achievement for a woman of that time. She lived and worked most of her life on the Dominicans' motherhouse campus, which included school buildings for kindergarten through high school and some dormitory space. Every two or three years, my family drove to Grand Rapids to visit her or she visited us in Western New York. Even today, when I hear a train whistle, I feel a lurch in my chest and recall vividly the sights, noise, even the smells of the grand, historic Buffalo Central Terminal. I remember passing the statue of a buffalo which towered over our heads, walking down to the tracks to meet her, bringing her home, taking her places, having meals together, responding to her requests for our kid stories.

While kindergarten was her lifelong passion, she also taught courses in sociology and education at St. Thomas Aquinas College on an adjacent campus. She believed strongly in the pivotal place of story, the arts, and building interpersonal and tactile skills in early education. Soon into her teaching career, she consulted to a design and construction team in building what became a special place on the campus. Designed as a "cottage" in the woods, Blessed Imelda Kindergarten was built with children in mind, inside and out. It was surrounded by a picket fence with arbored gate. Cats, chipmunks, squirrels, and occasionally, a pony roamed about, often gaining entrance through the gate. Inside, it seemed like the woods and winding paths came through the windows of the single open-space classroom. An indoor stone pond held goldfish, turtles, frogs, and nearly invisible tiny water creatures. Her pet dog, "Flicka," roamed about, entering and leaving through a small window with a swinging door, a dog-jump's length above the ground. The kitchen featured low counters and sink, refrigerator and stove at standard height; it contained everything for fixing a simple meal or snack. Its window also served as a gate into a cage for the pet rabbit who was free to come and go during the day. The weight-bearing columns in the classroom were encircled by low attached tables with chairs drawn round, seeming to encourage independent work. There were defined interest areas – terrarium gardens, small animal habitats, books and writing materials, easels in unexpected spaces, circles of chairs. The upright piano was open at all times. There was so much to see and hear. I harbored a secret wish that I could be one of the lucky children in such an oasis, that I could escape my simple rural milieu and be *there* some five hundred miles west, while at the same time not leaving my close-knit family and country school with seven grades in one room. I also remember fearing that the dream might fail me, that my yearning for unfaltering appreciation might not occur. Over time, the dream faded away. I enjoyed my one-room school education through seven years, went into the city for high school, and excelled academically.

Aunt Agnes retired from teaching in her early seventies. Whole generations of children and young people had passed through Blessed Imelda Kindergarten, many of them later holding leadership positions in their respective communities. Meanwhile, she joined us for family weddings and special occasions and we visited her several times. She lived to ninety years of age. Over her lifetime, local newspapers carried occasional testimonies from former students. Many of us were disappointed that her gifts to the world were barely mentioned at her funeral.

In retrospect, my correspondence with her from childhood on, family visits and my own visits as an adult, and, in some fashion, just thinking about these things became a kind of "north star." I did, in fact, shape my self-perceptions and important life decisions with her views in mind. While I can point to other influences, she taught sociology, I became a social worker, including working closely with children and youth in a settlement house. She completed a master's degree in education, I in public health. She could make anything grow, knew scores of wild plants by name and their husbandry, often engaging in little conversations with, or about, wildlife who crossed her path. Even into high school, I spent hours at a time roaming woods and forest, becoming keenly aware and committed to saving natural habitat wherever possible. I continue to enjoy gardening, though now I prefer deck gardens and perennial plantings, and protecting space for nesting robins. She was comfortable with the great Dominican writers and other theologians; I enjoy a broad range of spiritual writers and honing my own spiritual life. Children have always been a major part of my life, professionally and personally, especially, my multi-generation step-family, my nieces and nephews and their children.

Aunt Agnes' encouragement to observe and express myself creatively became central to my love of writing. It is there that I have always put my "self"—like a fingerprint. Today, I touch the framed image and allow a passing mind-play: if we had lived closer to each other, would she have continued to foster my creativity and the slow unfolding of my inner self? understood and soothed the setbacks? celebrated the milestones and triumphs?

I've aged enough to know it doesn't matter.

## First Tools

In the rural regularity of my childhood,
September meant new pencils, occasionally
a box of them with a sliding cover that fit
in a tin lunchbox.
                        It meant
the smell of wood—scraping thin shavings
that curled and broke into piles on the table,
shaping pencils to perfect points.
                        It meant
moving on to the next grade, more to learn,
a new desk, field trips to the woods, rolled-up
maps pulled down to eye level.
                        Even now,
September evokes a yearning to begin anew,
set aside things of little use, return to unread
books and untried intentions,
sharpen my focus.
                        This morning,
I am at my desk with #2 pencils, a pile of them.
Seven inches, end to end, sturdy, gift of forest
and hard labor, each one honed to a point.
I select one, cradle it in the crook
of my hand, poised for repair
and further invention.

## Etude for a Wildflower

For all these years I've barely noticed you—
Lacy umbels
By the road, favored bloom of the Queen,
Esteemed by old Hippocrates
As a cure, to be sure,
For ills
Puzzling, prevalent, powerful.

II

Imagine humble fields of ancient bloom—
Lacy umbels
In the wind, standing tall by the path,
And in their midst Hippocrates
Has his say, holding sway
On ills
Visible, treatable, solvable.

III

She ruled a mere few years yet fame is hers—
Scotland    England
Did agree to become one in might;
Sweet lace, a chair, a garden loved
All attest to her crest.
Sad Anne—
Faithful queen, face serene, pain unseen.

*Notes: Queen Anne Lace (QAL) is a wildflower which thrives in even forbidding soils, sometimes in great masses. A member of the parsley family, known also as wild carrot ("daucus carota"), it is first described in the teachings of Hippocrates - as a plant having useful contraceptive qualities. QAL became a popular addition to private gardens in the 17th Century during the reign of Britain's Queen Anne. Uncertainty remains regarding how it came to be named after the Queen who endured as many as eighteen pregnancies, yet died childless.*

*Each stanza above contains this sequence of metric patterns in poetry: (Iambic pentameter, Trochaic Dimeter, Anapestic Trimeter, Iambic Tetrameter, Anapestic Dimeter, Spondee, Dactyl*

## Nesting Patterns

For three springs, it has been my pleasure to partner with two robins in their nesting routines. The back of my house features a sliding-glass door and wall lantern to the right of the door, a deck and generous yard. Two robins arrive at the lantern and set to nest-building. I assume they are the same pair because nothing changes, year after year, on their part or on mine. I first see them when they tap and preen in the glass pane near the deck floor. I keep a few feet between us and welcome them, aloud and repeatedly, a kind of sing-song-affectionate message without regard to whether they are hearing me or not. I tell myself it doesn't matter. We are friends, old friends, now that we are into our third season together. They set to work, complete the nest-building task and occupy the space quietly. And, despite my repeated assurances of their safety, they leave temporarily if I or someone else appears nearby.

Soon, there are one or more eggs. They share nesting duties, just sitting there, and I go on wondering about what they are thinking about. Do they feel secure, are they grateful? Do they know how many eggs she will lay in any given year? Do they have any expectations at all? It happens, usually, that some morning I am alerted to new sounds up there – small peeps, fluttering wings over the nest, and eventually, I see two or three small beaks. The parents fly from tree to tree, drop down for a quick dig in the yard, and return to the nest, dropping worms or insects into yawning beaks and the sound of what I assume is satisfaction, maybe gratitude. We go on together for a few weeks, sharing our space and aging in place. The babies mature and, usually out of my sight, leave the nest. The rest is their own story.

One year later, in late June, I return to this essay. Three days ago, two robins were back at the door, tapping and preening as I've come to expect. And, once again, I reassured myself that these are my old friends. But this time, there was a problem. They worked at nest building, morning to evening, but their "stuff"—weeds, leaves, last season's forgotten pieces of garden string, small sticks and branches—piled up on the deck despite their repeated efforts to carry material up to the lantern and try again. I suspected one problem may be a very dry spring season, making soft mud harder to find, a texture required for weaving together the nest itself and affixing it reliably to the lantern. (My previous post-nesting-season -climb up the ladder to see for myself has left me in awe of their manufacture.) Both robins disappeared. I consulted with the Baltimore Woods Nature Center. They confirmed my suspicion and commended my stewardship.

I found myself saddened by the robins' disappearance, even questioning my own part in the story. Had I been invasive? too noisy? cleaned the lantern too thoroughly? I began to see  metaphors and connections to my own life experience. Is my space working for me, what occupies my life, how do I connect the pieces, make them worthwhile for myself or others? It can be like that when I'm writing a poem or essay—gathering words and lines from somewhere in my life experience, entering them on the page. I keep some material and weave them into the whole, others are either consigned to the margins for further invention or dropped altogether. I think of it like "literary architecture" where a project is designed, constructed, meets its purpose and is secured in place. Excellence is a matter of effort, learning, and, sometimes, the support of others who are, themselves, evidence of the art of stewardship.

**A Place of Her Own: A Trilogy**

I.  A Place of Her Own

This morning, a flurry of activity broke
the stream of light through the kitchen window,
just above the sash.  The robin was two-stepping
on the beam, barely missing the pergola lattice
overhead.  I stood at the sink, still.

She must have been at work since dawn.
Time after time, her mate flew from the woods
and a mid-way pause on a fencepost finial
to light on the beam, dropping mud,
dried grasses, stray garden twine and ribbon.
She tamped it into a soft surround, wove it
tight and secure.  By tomorrow,
only the top of her head will show.

I moved to my Queen Anne chair, upholstered
in robins and branches, and savored life
as I have known it—
framed photos, china in the corner cupboard,
St. Cecilia over the piano, a treasured Chagall,
the American Flag in a triangle box,
the shamrock wintered over, now blooming.

I turned my tablet to a new page and began to write—
jagged lines and smooth, words or whole ideas,
moving them up, down and around,
reading them aloud—searching
for shape and sound
and fit.

II.  Home, again

The robin's back—
same spot upon the beam.
She builds her nest in a day or two,
nestles into it, stretches the weave
and waits, perhaps dreams.

Oh, the certainty of it all!
Lay a few eggs, keep them warm until
they break open and hatchlings appear.
Drop slippery worms into their open beaks
day after day, until your task is complete.
Then, show them how to spread their wings
and find safe places… a kind of farewell.
I am comforted by her return, her trust in me,
the place I keep for her, as though it is a gift
to care for one another.

I scan this morning's news,
fret a little less about the day ahead.
I will glance up at the nest on the beam,
its tidy quiet, her head just above the rim,
and clean two rooms by noon.

III.  Morning Lessons

Yesterday, I watched you teeter
on the edge of the nest
before slipping back
among the others.

This morning, I saw you bounce
to the ground, hop a few steps,
fly to the garden fence
where the clematis trails
and rock yourself into balance,
your orange chest slowed
to a quiver.

I followed you, giving advice. Imagine that!
I tried to reassure you, urge you
to seek the low branches for now,
refine the tilt of your head,
your special view of things,
learn to sing and twitter,
fly with abandon.

There is no going back, you know.
Your life is now your own to shape.
Every nest is yours to arrange,
every worm yours to find,
every flight yours to take—
on still air or scolding winds.

I watched you fly away, past the pine tree.
It came to me that intimacy is a gift,
whether known or not. I want to think
you were the eldest as was I,
that it was time to leave,
that you will remember
this place,
          your family, me.

## Struggling Haiku

I come upon her
in the tall grass, not moving,
one leg folded back.

Shall I rescue her,
ease her pain and throbbing heart,
send her home again?

All else fades but this:
how best serve a wounded bird,
no plea rises clear.

Ah! Water will do—
elixir in a small dish,
sweet, a cure for sure.

Tip toe back, kind nurse,
(Francis was right: Here is love!)
guard every drop.

Alas, she is gone,
no adieu in the tall grass…
did she heal or flee?

**en plein air**
  *after a painting by Jeanne Dupre*


so strong the eagle's flight
wings full-spanned
splashed up
from watery catch
undisturbed by
hissing insect nests on muddy shores
soft rustling of ancient fir and pine barely hid
in shifting scrims of fog and misty rain

so swift the eagle's flight to lofty citadel
keeping faith with destiny
and a new generation
unaware of fame or artist's brush

# Connections

I rely on a Jitterbug Smart 3 android phone when out and about. Lively is the manufacturer. The company advertises with full page ads, often in spaces appealing to older populations. When asked about my choice, I hesitate to call it by name. Why has the company called it a "Jitterbug," as in the dance craze of my youth? Am I supposed to feel more comfortable with that image? It doesn't dance nor is it particularly lively, except for some ring choices. It is not juvenile nor am I. The company must know my age. I answered that question when I signed on five years ago because the price point and service were all I needed. It felt like leaving Verizon in the dust. I have added the app for Lively's urgent response system, signified by a star in a box, bottom right of screen. A caveat before continuing: I prefer my Verizon land phone (three jacks) for conversation, comfort and optimum hearing and keep this number listed in our community phonebook. I rue the growing disappearance of this practice, something which I fear can weaken the interpersonal fabric of a community.

So, it was with the Jitterbug in my pocket that I set out today on my morning walk, always a good way to think about things—issues, memories, decisions. Having just watched CNN coverage of conflicts and war in the Middle East and Israel, their stories, their lives seemed both close-up, and obviously, on the other side of the world. Not knowing what else to do, I prayed, asked God to somehow intervene and alter the course of this awful conflict. I saw people on phones, weeping, struggling to hear, to find images on their screens, holding them high toward the sky. Taking account of my phone close to my hip, and having begun writing these memoir essays, I fell in to sorting out my own personal "telephone history." I grew up in a very rural area and we had no house telephone until I was seven or eight years old. It was a "party line," meaning three or four families shared the same number with calls identified by the number of rings heard. You had to pay attention. Occasionally, Mother listened in on conversations, as did her friends and neighbors who admitted to the infraction. We children were allowed limited calls with friends which was not a problem since not all local families installed the service. I remember visiting the telephone company office in a neighboring town. The switch-board occupied one wall. One lady sat on a stool and connected calls by removing a plug from the caller's spot on the board and inserting it into the hole assigned to the receiving party. It worked well as long as there was power, a match between size of board and number of users, and number and length of conversations.

Think Lily Tomlin in popular comedy sketches of the 1960's and re-runs where, seated on a similar stool, she managed and messed up connections, occasionally entering a conversation herself. Smiling into the mouthpiece and speaking ever so carefully, she would say, "Is this the person to whom I am speaking?" Even on re-runs, that piece still evokes laughter from audiences, some of whom remember the truth of the scene.

Things got better. Telephone technologies advanced and we went on to a private line, no neighbor conversations to interrupt or listen in on. We family members were charged with taking down messages reliably for one another, a practice not so necessary today when most people - young and old - have their own hand-held phones, no need for message taking. There were telephone booths on street corners and other public places, sometimes with a folding door. I did not have my own access to a private phone until I had finished college and was living in an apartment. There was one memorable period when I was twenty-three years of age when I went bicycling and hosteling, alone, in the British Isles and travelling on public transportation in Ireland. Back then, it was uncommon for American women to take on such a trek: seven weeks completely separated from international telephone service except for a few transatlantic calls from American Express offices. It was a remarkable time for me—sites visited, roads taken, challenges met. I don't recall missing a telephone, although I noticed their public presence housed in windowed red booths with folding doors.

In the early 2000's, I was housing a young violinist who was performing around the United States and in our local summer music festival. She wanted to know about *me*, what had I done with *my* life, before I was living *here*—widowed, enjoying family, friends, a social life. She really wanted to know, even delayed leaving in order to have the conversation. I will never know why but I told her a short version of my 1963 bicycling and hosteling journey— not a "trip," I realized in the telling, but a "journey." She queried me repeatedly about how I stayed connected with others. "How did you manage? How did you get along without a phone in your pocket? Weren't you scared?" I was surprised by her investment in not moving on without my answer. I hadn't thought about it in exactly that way. There were tears in her eyes and in mine.

## The Word Is Out
*Fourth Iteration Since 2005*


There once was a box, tall and thin,
with panes of glass, a narrow seat, a
folding door to close us in. There, we
withdrew to make a call or two,
confine conversation to a very small
space—a booth, now rarely seen. It's
been exchanged for a cell. Eschewing
the privilege of privacy, we make our
calls on the move.  In cars, trains and
airplanes. Walking, running with dogs,
rushing carts down grocery aisles, and
resting on sand or grassy knolls. The
urgency to connect compels dialing
up, responding to rings, blinks, vibra-
tions in pockets. As though we are in
a private place like the tall thin box
with the folding door, our focus fixed
on hand-held screens while fingertips
slide through text, tapping on icons
that open like gates to other worlds…
Imagine horizons shrinking to a grid
across the sky, reframing the notion
of universe, the geography of mind.

**Postcard From Cuba**
**July 20, 2016**

Streetscape crowding out the sky
blue like the sea,
mural on a crumbling wall—legendary Che,
eyes straight on, beret, bearded, forever young.

Precious limited time—folks gathering to sit
on sidewalk curbs, phones and laptops in hand,
sharing WI-FI wafting down from an invisible grid
empowering fingers, conversation, connections.

Blue Chevrolet, kept alive these sixty years,
windows down, *Rumba Cubana* on the dash—
drums, claves, bass, voices and dancing feet
fusing like vapors rising on warm air—

soul of a nation yearning to be its full self,
rid of revolutionary rhetoric and failed promise,
engaging the future, embracing their history,
these images, too, embedded in their story
and in mine.

## Of Time Zones and Boundaries


As daylight fades into lengthening night,
I am reminded of time passing,
its metrics measured in light and dark and
assigned to zones defined by ancient wisdom.

I am reminded of coming winter, holidays and holy days,
a time to believe, hope, love more abundantly
wherever we are, the spaces we occupy, our tables set—
colors and aromas, platters piled high, corks removed,
our voices raised wherever two or more are gathered
and inclined to sing, chant, celebrate, let candles burn down.

I think of those serving the nation in every part of the world,
themselves confined to plated rations, a seasonal menu.
I think of families, old folks, young ones and babies
huddled in the detritus of bombings and battles fought
in cities, villages and deserts across multiple zones,
or crossing rivers and forests, mountains and minefields,
living under floorboards and useless vehicles,
in rubble and tented spaces or open fields,
their rations served from shoulder satchels and steaming pots
on to chipped plates and cups and waiting open hands.

I think of them, all of them,
fleeing devastating days and nights for a better life,
redefining courage, claiming their histories, their cultures,
raising their faces and voices on handheld screens,
signaling to a digital grid across the sky, no boundaries.
I think of them, all of them,
unnamed, unseen, until brought to light
through a camera's lens or a writer's voice.
I must look again,
not away.

# When Adventure Meets Purpose

Someone once asked me, "What is the bravest thing you have ever done?" I shy away from such "superlatives." Like others, I could list several "brave" moves over my lifetime. But the experience I describe here does stand out when I ponder the question. The reader will find references to this story elsewhere in this *Second Looks* collection.

In 1963, having completed three and one-half years at my first professional job (Charles Settlement House, Rochester, NY), I was bored, saw little opportunity for advancement, and was disappointed in my overall social life. I decided I needed change, in fact, a complete overhaul. That is, I needed to shape my life on my own terms, test my personal strengths, explore new ideas and experiences. I needed to get away, but somewhere safe. I had saved enough money to do something extraordinary. I decided to embark on a solo trip, go where I would know no one, rely on myself, get a grip, do something interesting. I chose the British Islands and Ireland where language and culture would not negate my purpose. I planned to be gone for perhaps two months, travelling alone, bicycling and hosteling, maybe a bed and breakfast now and then. It seems a little quaint now, but such decisions were uncommon for American women of that time. I made this decision against almost total negative feedback from family and friends. It took courage, tenacity, and hope. I researched possible itineraries and travel options, framing it all as an adventure. I covered rent in advance for the apartment I shared with two other women.

I set out, boarding a bus for New York City, passport in hand, but no ticket, just trust I could make it happen. Upon arriving at the harbor, I learned the Rotterdam was set to sail, but no tickets were available. I was devastated, went down to the wharf, sat on my bag and cried. Suddenly, the gangplank lowered with a thud on the pavement. The bursar ran down and told me a double berth room had become available because two American women had not arrived to claim their stateroom. We ran up the gangplank, I bought round-trip passage, and settled in. I was both scared and excited. I just sat on one berth and let my mind take in what had just happened. Slowly, I ventured out and got to know the ship, went to the first meal served in the dining room where we were all assigned our places for all meals. Seasickness came over me by early evening and took a couple days to conquer, mostly by taking advice of ship staff to just go to a railing and stare out at the dark sea. The Atlantic crossing took about seven days, during which time I studied maps, brochures, the British money system and niceties, and socialized at mealtimes and activities. It was like settling in, just the beginning. As I try to remember details, I find that daily ship life is a mental blur for me, even when I stare at the only picture I have from that voyage.

We debarked at Southampton, a city still bearing the awful devastation of World War II, still full of rubble and fallen buildings. I stayed there three days, enjoying a small bed and breakfast, exploring the city. I sent my larger bag to a storage locker in London which I determined would be a major locus for segments of my journey through England. As I did throughout my time on land, I spent time falling apart in fear and talking myself out of it, going out for meals and sightseeing and local social events. Most importantly, I bought a three-speed bicycle—considered advanced at that time— and a poncho. The latter was essential for traveling in all kinds of weather. I set out with just a sturdy small bag on the bike and a backpack.

I don't remember now the routes I traveled, but when on the road I biked about thirty miles a day. Fixing some simple meal in a hostel kitchen and small shared dormitory rooms meant meeting young people from all over the world. We residents were assigned housekeeping tasks every morning before heading out. Rain or shine, always with a poncho, you had to leave. Once, in a heavy windy rain, my poncho actually billowed out so that my bike and I lifted off the pavement. I remember biking through the hills and dales of the Lake Country, fabled home of famous writers of the British canon, around Oxford and Cambridge, the roads down to Dover and little places along the northern edges of Wales. And, of course, several days in London; I stayed there two days with friends of friends in the States. I took my bike on a train up to Glasgow and Edinburgh. Eventually, I set sail for Dublin across the Irish Sea and travelled around Ireland for over a week, absorbing that country's unique culture, beauty, and relationship to my Irish ancestry.

This adventure, so to speak, was not a trip. It was a journey in the most profound sense of that word. I learned so much about myself, tested myself with people and experiences, broadened my sense of who I was, who I could be, tried out different "selves," considered again what I might do with my life. I was never threatened and whenever I opened a map, someone came by to help me. Gradually, I became very much at peace.

Not having thought about it when I left New York, my passage ticket was round-trip, no refund for change. So, seven weeks later, in early November, I rode to Cork to board the Rotterdam and sold the bike. It was an extraordinarily cold stormy night and raining hard. We had to go to the ship by dingy and I was petrified. I don't swim. I remember climbing out of the dingy, on to a ship ladder, and hoisting myself up from the last step on to the ship floor. Thinking about it now, that seems metaphorical, like moving on to the next phase in my life journey. The one-week passage home was enjoyable. I met a voice coach who was sailing from Rome, hoping to try a new career as an "authentic Italian" voice coach in America. He gave me voice lessons off the back of the ship and I learned my first aria there – Mimi's aria, "Si, mi chiamano Mimi." Somehow, these rudimentary voice lessons strengthened a nagging urge I had had for a long time to study voice. After returning home, I applied as a special student at the Eastman School of Music in Rochester and studied there for two years. That opened a new door and I continued voice lessons for a few years, giving solo recitals from time to time, and singing in an orchestral chorus and performing small roles in local opera theater.

This story seems to qualify as an "adventure," certainly in its etymological sense. Surely, I was venturing toward an object or objective, with uncertainty about its ultimate resolve. Beyond doubt, it resides in the writer's memory as an essential piece of her life trajectory.

## Bouquet, 1963

The Rotterdam lay at anchor,
its gangplank rising steadily into place.
Farewells swirled up over railings and faded away.

Alone on the dock, a young woman sat
on her leather satchel, unzipped
at one end, enough for a small bouquet

to breathe there. A larger bag was at her side.
Head down, face sheltered under a brimmed hat,
tears escaped onto shirt and shoes,

her still knees.  She leaned forward, rose
to her feet and paused, picked up both bags
and walked toward the street, bent into herself.

Suddenly, the gangplank lowered, hit the dock, hard.
A ship's officer rushed to her side and spoke briefly.
She nodded, pulled her passport from the satchel,

surrendered it to him, and smiled. He took her bags
and they ran up the laddered plank, disappearing
into the ship's wide portal

and a new chapter,
setting boundaries and letting go,
                         another country.

**Self Talk, A New Place…**
*After Edward Hopper, Automat 1927*


I came up on the train today.
This is my wish, my dream, my tears disappearing
into the rain sliding across the windows.

Everything I know passes behind me, out of view—
wetlands of tall grasses and cattails,
geese resting before their long journeys,
barns and rooflines made for each other fading away
into houses with small yards backed up to fences by the tracks,
smoke stacks and streetscapes crowding out the sky.

The train's brakes slow us out of the wind, its underbelly
groaning and clanging, loud and insistent.
We lurch to a stop.
People are getting off and on,
chasing dreams or sleepwalking through another day.

We're moving again, faster, faster.
A lone whistle trails behind us, sighing into the wind,
mysterious yet knowing, like a keeper of tales, mine, too.

Dropping speed, we screech through another tunnel,
then under the station roof with its broad bed of tracks, my stop …
nothing like where I have been but where I am now, where I will be.
I must take it all in, let it become a part of me,
how I will walk and talk and carry myself.

I take this table near the door, a straight-back chair, cross my knees.
Where shall I set my eyes, my hands, my yellow chapeau?
Can I make this work?
Will the power of the dream hold me,
enfold me, sustain me, here, in this new place?

# Evelyn's Gift

Only the shell remains of the goose egg, cracked open on one side in a perfect oval, everything intact. But that's the bare minimum of how I think about this perfectly crafted work of art created by my friend and neighbor, Evelyn, herself confined to a wheelchair, her hands hobbled by arthritis. She gave it to me it to me thirty some years ago in honor of our friendship. Evelyn had stitched tiny pearl beads in perfect rows, covering the entire surface, minus the opening. The interior "wall" or surround is covered in paper—an illustrated garden for a small gray and white bird who sits on a nest and stares out at any onlooker straight in the eye. Evelyn glued the egg to a three-legged brass holder and set it on a small plate inside a clear dome. Nothing touches it—not wind, nor heat, nor ice, not even chatter nor music nor bird calls at my patio door.

Evelyn and her husband David lived across the street from my husband and me in Brookeville, Maryland, a small colonial market village situated on a busy state highway. They had lived in and around Brookeville all their lives and were well known for their love of local history and all things World War II. They were respected keepers of antiques, collectibles, and highly regarded crafts and crafting materials. Both our homes were occasionally on historic property tours. Evelyn had suffered polio as a child and multiple falls and fractures in her adult years. She  operated her electric wheelchair independently and with grace. She taught me to drive her adapted van, and we went to stores, meetings, special events, wherever we desired. Evelyn was  an activist for rights of the disabled, including being involved in the creation and passing of the Americans With Disabilities Act (July 29, 1990). So it was that she, and therefore, I, were invited to the U.S. Capital for the signing of the Act, an exciting opportunity for both of us. We parked the van in a designated place and got inside easily. Evelyn's chair allowed her to control the height of the seat, so we "stood" side by side, head near head. In addition to all the senators, representatives, and other notables in attendance, there were people with every kind of disability, along with their companions. There were hundreds of us – on chairs, walkers, portable narrow beds. There were people with hearing or sight disabilities, others with various cognitive and emotional challenges. You could sense the hope and anticipation in the room. The Disabilities Act changed life for all Americans, our comings and goings. Think adapted sidewalks at curbs, designated vehicle parking, signage in braille, ramps and elevator design, requirements in public housing and architecture. *Everyone should and can be included*—that was the point.

Energized by this experience, Evelyn and I continued to advocate for rights of the disabled and for governmental and public support to address dangerous traffic issues through our village. We also began to advocate for various ways to celebrate our village's coming 200th birthday. After much thinking and dreaming, we moved on to what was for us a daring goal. We proposed to our town government that we would co-chair a "Brookeville Bicentennial Planning Committee" in preparation for the two-hundredth year of the village's founding in 1794. They agreed, although with hesitation, if not trepidation. Central to that plan was the cooperation of county and state government transportation agencies to support re-direction of public traffic through the village for at least one day, something that had never happened in the village's two hundred years. This required several meetings with state, county an3 village officials, mostly held in the Brookeville Academy, situated right there on the busy highway through town.

Together, Evelyn and I were formidable, maybe awesome. We presented our case and what we hoped to do. We didn't argue, didn't back down. After three meetings, these folks began to see what we saw. It was agreed: the state highway through the village—about one mile of it—would be closed for one day— September 10, 1994—from early morning to 6pm. It was not lost on any of us that this would require extensive traffic control planning to accommodate what was roughly a thirteen-mile state highway. In the end, the Brookeville Bicentennial became a weekend celebration, September 9-11, 1994. It featured a homecoming reception, parade, house tour, music and entertainment, games, food, even a giant cake with icing made to look like the United States flag, free pieces to all! It was an event larger than most people had anticipated. Official estimates put the crowd that day at 4,000 visitors, in a village of perhaps two hundred residents. As 6pm approached, traffic police on duty were themselves reluctant to re-open the road in view of the remarkable celebration that had taken place and would be continuing into the following day.

I need only look at Evelyn's remarkable artistry or show it to visitors to be thankful for our friendship and the lessons I learned along the way. My husband and I retired and moved to Central New York in January 1999 in order to be near our family. Evelyn passed away in 2006. We returned for her funeral. I wheeled my husband in his transport chair to the hillside cemetery entrance and participated in the service from that viewing spot. Writing this essay has served to remind me, once again of the delicate and intricate process of weaving friendship and accomplishment into our life journeys and sense of self, and on the other side, mourning the loss of those treasured relationships. Now in my ninth decade of earthly life, Evelyn's crafted gift stands in for the larger gift – the power of companionship, sharing sometimes "big" ideas, wrestling down moments of doubt, and moving on to victories like that reflected in the gift which inspired this essay.

*NOTE: This essay followed a writing prompt the writer offered to two newly housed/formerly homeless persons who were exploring their writing interests and abilities. Prompt: "Describe something among your possessions now and why it matters to you." The writer set about answering the prompt herself.*

# Mrs O'Flaherty's Kitchen and Beyond

Last evening, the moon was glorious, low in the sky, a perfect orb in orange-gold like a ball riding free on still night air, over fields, hills and lake. I felt lifted up, compelled to connect like I might with an old friend. Pausing at turns on the narrow road and shifting views through the trees, I found myself wondering at what seemed the evocative here. A memory began to unravel…

*of the moon, an Irish woman, a knitted hat, and my husband and me sitting in Mrs. O'Flaherty's cottage kitchen on the island of Inishman, off the coast of Galway, some fifty years ago. A deep-set window, its lace curtain pulled back to the frame, offered views of multiple greens, stone-fenced fields, hints of sea clouds—all cast in the island's fabled light. Having lingered over a final hearty breakfast, we joined Mrs.O'Flaherty who was knitting an Aran hat for me. A transistor radio crackled overhead. I asked if she had heard about Neil Armstrong's recent walk on the moon. She looked up, amused. Yes, she had heard, but who would believe it? She cited her years of acquaintance with the moon. It was clear, she declared. No one could have walked upon it.*

*Later that year, Marshal McLuhan was on a lecture circuit offering a controversial theme: Armstrong might never have walked on the moon. Maybe it took place in a well-equipped television studio, enhanced with the latest media technologies. Entirely possible, McLuhan claimed.*

Even now, occasionally, all these years later, on a clear night with the moon full and high overhead, I remember that moment in Mrs. O'Flaherty's kitchen, our chat about the moon. I follow its celestial path over my house, window to window. No sign of footprints. I think about my treasured Aran Islands hat, tissue-packed and resting in a small oval hat box with fitted lid. And I am reminded of the many sides of truth.

# Moonscape

*Tomorrow, half past seven, Eastern Daylight Time,*
*the moon will suffer a blow on its south pole. An*
*empty two-ton rocket propelled at six thousand*
*miles per hour will pierce the darkness of the*
*Cabeus crater, looking for water or ice, a finding*
*signaled by a giant plume of lunar dust and*
*captured on cameras and sensors linked*
*to websites and monitors on earth.*
*~Adapted from The Post-Standard, "Shoot the moon,"*
*  11/08/2010*

I've known your face all my life,
sometimes in full view or the lake
or arcing across my roof,

sometimes disappearing behind trees
or a moving layer of sky, losing girth,
becoming a sliver, a shadow
but there, always there.

How will I know you survived?
Will your features shift, your mouth droop
a little to the right or the left, your eyes seem half closed?
Or will you feel anything at all?

This will not be the first time we've landed
on your craggy surface, left debris, footprints.
This time, though, we will have entered.

**Beach Theater: A Play Without Words, Almost**

*It is just past midnight. They enter on a narrow path,*
*through shadowy sea pines and clumps of dried dune grass,*
*their feet sinking into the sand bleached white. They keep*
*their voices low, spread out over the nearly empty beach.*
*Down the shore, shadowy figures lean in to a campfire.*

Like filament wires spindling across the Gulf,
wave crests edge to shore, patter on to the beach,
spill around footprints, shells, a turtle back.

Diana, stark white to her edges, hangs low
overhead.  Mistress of the sky tonight.
Stars, everywhere – brilliant, quivering
behind distant scrims.

*They pull i-phones and droids from their pockets*
*and frame whole constellations, sand to sky, and cry...*

"Yes, yes, there they are!"
The galaxies Orion and The Dippers,
enchanting, reliable, fixed in memory
and on screens…

*It is 1:35am. Silence. Eyes on the moon.*

A round shadow creeps over the left side, just
a sliver, and continues on, recasting the moon
in true red. A thin corona glows around her rim.
The shadow exits right and disappears.

There's something primitive in the universe
tonight, something intimate yet beyond reach.

*It is 2:45am. They stand in the dark, reluctant to leave,*
*then exit slowly on the same path, their voices low.*

*Note on the Solstice:  On December 21, 2010, for the first time in 400*
*years, the earth eclipsed the moon, a moment of extraordinary intimacy.*

## Friend Come Calling

I've been waiting for you, Strawberry Moon,
both of us living out our cycles and days in sync—

you, riding steady on the night air
      above the trees and quiet streets,
      across my window, left to right,
      your path and pace ordained
      by cosmic forces beyond my knowing,

while I, lying here
      on this narrow bed and thin mattress,
      healing, hopelessly awake, am assured
      by your passing this night,
      our brief conversation.

# Why Funerals Matter

Recently, I attended a funeral for a well-known person. The pews were full to overflowing, flower arrangements were placed strategically, chatter was subdued, the service was conducted with care and affection. Distracted by sunlight flooding the tall window near my pew, I read the donor names inscribed at its foot. Who were they, what did they do with their lives, were their funerals held in this same space? As I returned home, I wrestled with a question: "Why do funerals matter?" or "Do they matter?" It was as though I had left the event but the event had not left me. Funerals, in any formal or historically familiar fashion, seem to be disappearing from our everyday life. Relatedly, environmental concerns and personal preferences are increasingly pivotal in decisions and management of body remains.

I grew up knowing about funerals—what happens, why we go to them. My mother was a strong believer in being with people at times of death, occasionally taking food to a grieving family. She took us, even as young children, to many wakes and funerals, whether they were for family or acquaintances. Our cousin was an undertaker and I remember their gracious "funeral home," the high ceilings, heavy fabric drapes, upholstered straight back chairs. I remember learning how to behave in this setting and handle the awkwardness any child might feel. Sometimes, we were invited out to the family kitchen for a snack or to see how calls for ambulance services came in over the short-wave radio.

Going to wakes, calling hours, funerals and comparable services, helping to host post-funeral receptions, and watching televised state funerals and memorial events have been a regular feature of my life. I watched the grand "lying in state" event in the United States Capitol rotunda for Rosa Parks and the thousands of people who waited silently in long lines to file past her coffin. I was moved to write *"Woman in the Window,"* a poem included in an anthology published in connection with the 200th anniversary of Abraham Lincoln's birth. I have come to see that a funeral service, thoughtfully and lovingly executed, calls us to stop our busy lives and take measure of this person, the "now departed." We sift through private and public biographies, treasured moments and lost opportunities to honor this person, however talented or feeble our testimony. We may err on the side of exaggerating the qualities of the deceased, but, over time, balance will return and closure can begin. Folding these memories and insights into our own ongoing paths to personal growth allows us to cherish this person and bid farewell. In some faith communities, the prayers, music, and liturgical actions speak eloquently and with compassion to the belief that a funeral is both a "rite of communion" and a "rite of passage." We are called to blend our affection and grief in a spirit of intimacy with the deceased. We pray for the departed and for ourselves and look again at the meaning of life. We are reminded of God's promise of eternal happiness for all. In the same spirit, we are invited to see this parting as a rite of passage which is both beautiful and mysterious. In some traditions, near the end of the service, the celebrant and choir intone, "May the angels lead you into paradise…" I love this line. Even now, I cannot resist imagining the angels leading our "dear departed" into paradise—halting or steady, fearful or brave, maybe clad in some characteristic fashion. But make no mistake. I dread death, either my own or those I love, and this reality does not disappear by a call to prayer or a song or funny story. Being truthful to my roots and what I have learned through the years, I frame that farewell in the context of a spiritual setting where faith and personal relationships are central to the event, and where love, tears, and laughter can enter in.

In quite a different take on the funeral which sparked this essay, I began to think about people who exit this world with hardly a nod. What about migrants and refugees who die on their journeys to a better life, whether on land or sea? What happens to homeless people in shelters or on the streets, the forgotten in jails and hospitals, the merely tolerated or left-alone among our families? Are they buried in caskets or urns, in marked or unmarked graves? Are they brought to a place of worship or public gathering for some rite of burial? Who come to mark their time on earth or pray that angels lead them into paradise?

## Woman in the Window: Remembering Rosa Parks

Today, she lies in state, a woman of uncommon grace.
She defied historic caveat and chose honor, not merely a place.

Famous now in windowed profile, she stared at everything,
at nothing, as though the bleak December day could bring

her strength, calm her beating heart, take away fear,
let the surpassing might of will dry any tear.

She must have known what lay ahead:
metal bracelets, a numbered photo, a narrow bed.

To all who heard that day, power spoke to power
and a mighty roar went up to claim that hour

for history, as wheels slowed and marching feet
in lock-step cadence stormed the streets.

Out of the long silence, ancient anthems rose
like armored battle cries turned on dreaded foes.

Slowly, a nation moved to meet the promise
of its founding dream and those who bore it final witness.

Today, she lies in state, coffined in a marble hall,
while footsteps fall in solemn lines, a requiem for all.

No simple woman here, she of few words and abundant hope,
who held a nation to account, her life beyond the camera's scope.

***Note:**  Rosa Parks died on October 24, 2005.  Her brave action on December 1, 1955 became a pivotal historic moment in the Civil Rights Movement.*

## The Long Arc of a One-Room School Education:
## A Teacher, a Library Book, and a Stay at Hull House

Mrs. Robinson, our teacher through grade school, was a remarkable woman, now that I think about her. Gray hair swept up at the back of her head in a rolled-over knot, a smart, caring woman. But it was her no-nonsense-affect that I remember today. I was one of her students through the 1940's. There were about thirty of us, seven grades in one room. Just imagine that. Every now and then, she would simply announce that we were closing down and going to the woods to explore nature. In retrospect, maybe she just needed a well-deserved break. It was on one of these visits to the woods that I discovered the Jack-in-the-pulpit wildflower standing under a tree. Books were few, so every two or three weeks she drove seven miles to the public library and picked up a supply of books for us, enough that they fit exactly on one of the wide window shelves. We could borrow them at will.

One day, I picked up a novel (whose title I have forgotten) about a Czechoslovakian family who had emigrated recently and settled in Chicago. One daughter was about my age, Anna her name, and she was the major narrator in the family's story. While I learned about the great effort it took to emigrate and settle in America, I was fascinated by their frequent experiences at Hull House in urban Chicago. Think of it as a community center located in the heart of a city with multiple immigrant communities. The whole family went there, not always together. They attended day or evening classes and events – English language and citizenship classes, sewing, crocheting and dressmaking groups, woodworking and mechanical skills workshops, music lessons and/or small music ensemble playing groups. Anna played the violin. To me—a country school kid living miles away from anything resembling urban— this sounded heavenly. After school, I simply walked home every day to our country home, small quarters but comfortable, but no interesting stuff to do like Anna experienced.

I stored away the memories and went on to further schooling. I went to college and earned a Baccalaureate degree in Sociology and Pre-professional Social Work. My first job, September 1963, was at the Charles Settlement House in Rochester New York. We served a largely first and second-generation Italian community and a growing first-generation Puerto Rican population. I was responsible for after school programming for kids – "fun in the arts," play-room, cooking classes. Adults came for evening classes in English, citizenship, discussions, etc. I realized that somehow I was now working in a place like the one Anna and her family went to regularly, and that seemingly miraculous connection deepened my sense of comfort in the position. About eighteen months later, my director offered me a remarkable opportunity: to attend a national settlement house conference at Hull House in Chicago, boarding at an attached rooming house. I was beyond thrilled. My first flight. All expenses paid.

I don't remember details of the conference, but I do remember visiting the classrooms, the woodworking labs, the gathering spaces. Most of us who attended were young, just entering the field of social work, paying attention to a new term back then—social justice. I don't remember how it happened, but there was also a small group of *Freedom Riders*—on break from their daunting struggles down south in the Civil Rights Movement. Their stories and testimonies, invitations and challenges to join the movement—even just attitudinally—remain as one of my valuable learning experiences. What I took away from the whole experience was not translated fully into programming at Charles House, but it surely confirmed what we were doing—in our kitchen, meeting rooms, woodworking lab, in our passion and affection for the people we were serving. I still believe that the settlement house movement—with all it has to offer to urban and immigrant communities—represents the absolute core of what social work is all about.

For me, Anna stayed close to me, like my own pretend-friend. And I played violin later in life on an old hand-me-down instrument, having lessons my father arranged with a co-worker, Mr. Smith, who was African American and came to our house to give me lessons. I let the lessons go after a year or two, until I enrolled as an adult "special" student in voice studies at the Eastman School of Music in Rochester, N.Y. Faculty urged me to also study violin for musical "ear-training"– always useful to a singer. So, the old violin came to use again. And I remembered Anna.

*Note: Hull House, founded by Jane Addams (and her friend, Ellen Starr Gates) in 1893 in Chicago, Illinois, served immigrant communities arriving in that city. It was the most famous and influential of the settlement houses of that time, and was, essentially, the earliest form of social work in the United States.*

### *Look.  It's a Jack-in-the-Pulpit!*


I went to my knees, the better to see
the tall green plant striped in purple and gold,
soft in my fingers like Mom's velveteen purse.

And look, said the teacher, there's the preacher
standing tall in the cup like a pulpit
with a roof overhead, not a word to be heard,

Quiet, little round head, still as can be,
as though waiting 'til we look and summon a friend
who lifts the soft roof, just a peek, looks again.

How did Jack get his name, we asked our teacher.
He doesn't look like any Jack we know, but still,
we like his name, the purples and greens.

We knew she would know. A very smart botanist
in far-away Sweden, some two hundred years ago,
got up very close to look and gave him his name.

-------

I no longer get down on my knees to see for myself.
I went to my screen. So much to discover,
it tires the brain. I hope my Jack lives well

this winter, stays safe from rabbits and deer.
Wait! Look what I found on line. Who knew?
*Jack's blossoms can change from male to female!*

So, be alert and in sync with the times:
You could call out distinctly, "How delightful
to meet once again, dear Jill-in-the-Pulpit."
It could be one or the other.

# Street Scenes

Occasionally, there are experiences in life, whether professional or personal, which strike a reflective note in the observer, where the characters or incidents effect a powerful emotional impact apart from the narratives per se. Capturing this inner reality in artistic form is compelling in its own right and further embeds the experience in memory. That is the genesis of this essay.

Many years ago, I was involved in a university-based research project which presented this opportunity. It consisted of nearly five-hundred interviews with men who had been diagnosed with a serious psychiatric disorder and had therefore experienced mental health services over a wide geographic area. Our purpose was to find them, talk with them to learn more about their life situations over recent years, improve diagnostic interviewing techniques, and refer them to services if indicated. Their involvement in the project was voluntary. My role was to locate these men, explain the project, and request their participation. This can be a transient population and finding them was challenging. I located eighty per cent of these men and seventy-five percent of them agreed to participate, most of them because they wanted to do something for others. "I'm glad I helped a little" were frequent last words. This comment has remained with me as the ultimate grace between human beings.

While there is often fear that people with serious mental health challenges are dangerous or to be avoided, I was never assaulted or threatened. In fact, I was more often struck by their seeming harmlessness, loneliness, and lack of meaningful interaction with their respective life situations.

On the few occasions when I thought there might be some altercation or danger, I did not pursue the interview. In today's world, it would probably not be possible to carry out such a project. Street drugs and firearms were not prevalent nor were they a contributing factor in the life situations of most of the persons I interviewed. However, their stories are still relevant. These were real people, trying to live out their lives in difficult circumstances. Their interactions remain with me as immensely valuable learning experiences. Among the hundreds of interviews I completed, I chose three that struck a responsive chord in me, leading me to reflect on what I learned there, edging closer to what I still see as universal truths playing out in the human experience, regardless of time and place. *Donna, Death of a Friend, and Finding Paul* are three of those essays. All names are fictional.

# Scene I:  Donna

This is not the story of Bruce, whom I had come to interview, but of his daughter, Donna. She was a child of few words, a flickering smile. She held her fingers high and told me she had  reached the age of four, soon to be five and "going to school." I looked from her to her father and wondered what school will be like for her. This family had sought little contact with neighbors or their own kin. They were well known to social and health services. Therefore, I knew something of their functioning on most social parameters, their educational experience, and Bruce's employment and court records. What may appear to be anonymity is not entirely, hardly ever.

But back to Donna. She wheeled a spanking new doll carriage up and down the length of the kitchen, carrying an old white summer purse on her arm, walking as though on a familiar street, ready to greet a familiar face. ((I remembered doing the same.) Meanwhile, we went on talking, her father and I. About him and the illness which plagues him—"the nervousness, the jumbled ideas." He reached across the breakfast-strewn table for a cigarette but the pack was crumpled and empty. He called to Donna and asked her to go to the store for a pack of Luckies. Willingly and silently, Donna wrapped herself up in cap and jacket. She waited for money to make the purchase, waited several minutes and never said a word. Then, she told her father she would need a note, this purchase by a four-year-old being against the law.

Donna returned in a few minutes, clutching a little brown bag with change jingling inside. Her father lit a cigarette and continued talking, thanking his daughter like an aside. She removed her cap and jacket, picked up her doll, and climbed on to a chair near where we were sitting. She pulled a crayon from her pocket, raised it to her lips, and flicked it slowly over her father's ash-tray. He smiled.

Donna was a lesson to me, perhaps a lesson in selective learning or the imprint of milieu. In that sense, there was a mark of universality about her—a child responding and living out patterns of culture, maturing as clearly and truthfully as her surroundings directed. I thought about my friends' young children, the academic and other skills they are developing, how they know how to change the colors of their dolls' hair, how to swim across a pool. But I doubted that any of them could boast of an accomplishment like Donna's on that winter day.

## Scene II:  Death of a Friend

Neil became acquainted with Bill, the intended subject of this interview, when both were patients on a hospital ward for alcoholics. Neil was discharged from the ward some time ago and took a room at this inner-city rooming house where I met him for this interview. A few weeks earlier, Bill was also discharged from the ward. Neil invited him to share his room at the rooming house until he could find something for himself. Bill died one week after moving in. The coroner's report was inconclusive. I was sent by project staff, at the request of the coroner's office, to learn more about Bill's death, specifically whether he might have taken his own life. There had been an upsurge in deaths of men with similar histories and this was of concern to the health services community.

Neil said that Bill's health in the days before his death seemed good, generally. "But he had a funny way of talking, you know. Not a stutter really, but he'd lose his words and have to start again. He was like that even in the hospital." He added that Bill only complained about a cold and a vague rib ailment in the week before his death. He took some pills regularly and worried if he misplaced them. He said Bill slept and ate more at the hospital than when they shared the room at this address. "He was a strange fellow. After a week, I had had it, you know. Well anyway, he gets a check for $25 from his mother in the morning and he says, 'I oughta go get some wine.' I tell him, just go down there to the corner and turn left a couple blocks. Do you know it took him two hours?  He got lost! He was always doing that, getting lost." On the day he died, Bill sat for two hours reading his mother's two-page letter. "I just couldn't stand it now.  It wouldn't take you or me that long to read it."

Then, Neil and Bill each consumed a bottle of wine and didn't leave the house again that day. Neil shut off the light about 9:00pm and was kept awake by Bill's heavy snoring. "I wanted to tell him to do something, blow his nose."  Finally, the snoring stopped and Neil soon put on the light again and found Bill as described later in the police investigation report. Neil sat on the edge of the bed and read awhile, adding that he had the "shakes" himself. "My God, he's dead!  I didn't have a dime to call the police so I waited 'til morning and the fellas thought I was joking." The landlady investigated and agreed. Neil made much of the snoring and added that he was told this was the fourth death in that room.

A week later, I returned to the scene and sat on the brick steps leading to the verandaed porch the autumn sun of late afternoon reached down to this asphalt place where the roar of heavy machinery signaled a new traffic loop which will shut off a street like this by a concrete barrier. I was waiting for Neil to return. The other residents told me he had gone to register to vote and visit the local bar. I snatched this time to read, and curiously enough, I had chosen a chapter on the aging from Edgar May's *The Wasted Americans*.

A tall and agile elderly man approached on the support of a cane. He asked me nicely who I had come to see. "He stopped for a couple beers. I'll get him. He won't mind." It was a warm sunny day and he had time to spare. I read on for a few more pages. Time seemed less important to me, too. The two men approached, unhurried, and we met again. I don't know if it was a typical time in the afternoon for residents to gather or if interest had been generated by my visit, but the veranda chairs were soon occupied and a few quiet conversations were underway.

Meanwhile, Neil and I sat on the brick steps and talked. Talked about what can't be taken lightly. A terribly human thing. Make no mistake, however. He never revealed strong sentiment about the event and I didn't know which was more contagious—his easy candor or my own frank statement of purpose and subsequent questions. Reflecting on this reality led to this essay. Here is what I mean. A man took pity on another man. He didn't really know him, the "Deceased," we call him. He could tell me little about him. And yet, that man died in *his* room. We can't ever uncover the realities of that night or the days before. It is best left to fiction. As we ended our talk, Neil returned to the room of which I had caught only a glimpse. Enough to sense the milieu of this autumn tale. I thanked him and he answered, "I hope I helped you a little." Knowing that he had helped to close the scant report and, more importantly, that he had provided an unforgettable lesson in compassion, bore him dignity. At least for that day on the brick steps.


"The only kind of dignity which is genuine is that which is not
diminished by the indifference of others.".
~D.Hammarskjold, *Markings*

## Scene III:  Finding Paul

Sometimes, one life story reveals the vast disconnect among person, health and health care, and that person's unique relationships to the community of which he or she is a part. It is ecology on the most micro of levels. This same disconnect only grows in chaos and pain when it is set against the ongoing renewal of urban communities in which tracts of land are rebuilt to suit new trends in commerce, public services, traffic management, and housing—becoming, thereby, the "new downtown." The publicity is plotted, ribbon-cutting rehearsed, and the return of a lively metropolitan area anticipated. And last, someone may ask, "Where will they go?" – the people who live in rooms and apartments above and along the streets and know these condemned blocks by heart. What about those who have shut out the world and know only the paths to their own doors, their own safety? And what about those who found a cheap place to live and didn't intend to stay here long? The stairwells go up and up and up to the homes of the people.


**Looking for Paul**

Paul was one of those people who had moved around the urban center, now a scene of "renewal." He had been diagnosed with alcoholism, depression (especially, after his wife's death a few years ago), social disengagement, perhaps a candidate for suicide. One brother knew he was alive but disavowed any marks of kinship. Another brother, himself in poor health, had only vague information about his whereabouts. Eventually, I found Paul in a small single-bedroom apartment house in the heart of the loop-cordoned area where he also was employed as a laborer in a service business. I asked him about his work. He complained a little about his responsibility and long hours, but he was also proud of himself. Besides, he said, "It's better than being lonely." He told me he sometimes opens a six-pack with other tenants to pass away the long evening hours. He loves classical music and listens almost nightly to his small FM radio.

From Paul's vantage point, "...the city's going downhill." He has watched people leaving, greatly diminishing the business of his employer. The "nice little park' is gone now, the place where he and his friends used to sit in the sun and visit and reshape the world to their own visions. Yes, he said, there will be another park in the renewal area, but it won't be the same. Overall, he seemed to be doing well.

**Looking For Paul, Again**

Fifteen months later, I returned to Paul's neighborhood where we had met. No one knew his whereabouts. His old employer called him "elusive." The new owners of his former place of employment did not recognize his name. Eventually, I learned that he had moved to a county home for the aged. When I arrived there, he ushered me to the men's section of the home. A forced cough from another resident heralded my new intrusion into male space. I wanted to learn what had brought him here, a man in his fifties. I also wondered what he thought about the changes in his former neighborhood.

Paul told a fairly disjointed tale of the past year. Though snow lay on the ground, it was autumn to this man who could not remember where he had been, only the "blackouts" and the vague recognition of having needed care. "Things kept happening to me...the fire...I lost my money, maybe I got rolled...I don't know." I asked him what he thought about the changes in his former neighborhood. He could not remember. What had the year been like for him? What happened to his FM radio? Names, dates, the sequence of events were all one vast piece of unknowing. In fact, a fire, the origin of which he only vaguely understood, had destroyed his apartment house and all of his belongings. The lawyer, whose name I recognized, answered one of Paul's calls, only to say that the restitution of property is a dragging thing. He did not feel the loss of a F-M radio. We sat down to talk. Paul told me he works a few hours a day in his new home, arranging meal trays for the residents. He complained a little about his responsibilities and long hours. However, he was proud of his role. "Besides, it's better than being lonely."


**Looking Elsewhere**

I was not satisfied. What really had happened during the past year? Agency records revealed visits to outpatient clinics and multiple brief psychiatric hospitalizations with scant information about events precipitating those admissions. There were repeated diagnoses of DTs and paranoia, and, typically, a discharge note, "... discharged...improved, disposition to self." A man alone, who cannot cope with himself. Friends and relatives were listed in only a perfunctory manner. They are not expected to come calling. The man himself can't remember. I could go no further, other than to write into my record, "Found at county home, seemingly comfortable." I wanted to add, disposition to self.

"Loneliness is not the sickness unto death. No, but can it be cured by death? And does it become harder to bear the closer one comes to death?"
~D.Hammarskjold, *Markings*


Author's Note: Being Alone, Being Self
Whatever had transpired for Paul over the past year, probably the years before, will go largely unknown. It isn't even a secret. I was reminded of a period of several weeks in my early twenties which I spent alone, bicycling and hosteling on the roads of Great Britain. It was a journey of personal discovery, some bravery. It was back when American women did not typically travel alone in this fashion. Back when there was no Internet or cell phone technology. Although I met many people along the way, no one knew about me or what had gone before, how that day was really part of yesterday and the beginning of tomorrow. While that privacy was a blessing—being occasionally so alone can be a good thing—that whole time is *my* secret which I alone may choose to relate. *But it is subject to recall*, and in that sense, it is real. I am privileged to consider my story "memoir."


"The longest journey is the journey inwards"
~D. Hammarskjold, *Markings*

# Short Breaths

*"Short breaths were all we had, he and I.*
*Just enough energy to face the next task, hope ever so slightly,*
*let the words flow out while calling from within a mammoth*
*effort to stifle tears and summon strength."*
Journal entry, May 2005


    *Short Breaths* combines narrative and poetry in a brief telling of our experience—my husband's and mine—with his non-traumatic brain injury or "stroke," modest recovery, final illness and death. This is a story about fear, loss, endurance, patience and impatience, kindness and love. It is not about remarkable medical interventions and diagnostic procedures. Medications and hospitalizations were the only available acute treatment options. For the most part, rehabilitation therapies were effective and delivered wisely and compassionately, although they were limited by insurance policies. In the midst of this turmoil and life style change, regular meetings with my writers group sustained my other life as a writer. One member gave me Basho's collection of haiku and prose, *Narrow Road to the Interior*. These brief verses, full of meaning and imagery riding through tightly crafted lines, inspired me to continue writing my own brief reflections. Following Basho's model, I designed and wrote *Short Breaths* to integrate narrative and poetry in a "haibun" format.

Our spring vacation in Florida had been both enjoyable and stressful, the latter occasioned by a lot of driving and heavy traffic, something which Al and I had eliminated from our lives since moving to Central New York. We returned home in April 2004, unpacked at a leisurely pace and tried to resume our usual activities. We soon recognized that he seemed more tired and confused, but hoped his strength would return with rest.

55

## Noticing Things

Where is his laughter,
his concern for me,
his prescient teasing?

Where is his living-life-large self
daring the edges, the voracious mind
seeking wisdom, sharing wisdom?

Where is his full body turn
folding me into the night's quiet,
embraced and safe?

On Monday morning, Al's symptoms had not abated. I called for an ambulance.


## First Signs

Sleep      not rest        heavy on his eyes
syllables  not words    shadows of a voice
familiar   feeble   fading too quickly

One hand hangs limp
unknowing
the other knows full well

His words fall across the page
dragging ink and thought
in wrinkly lines

Too long    It takes too long to cross the room
one step   then another   heavy   flat on the floor
a shuffled pace to the nearest chair

Light of crimson red
blinks and spins over speeding wheels
and eyes locked on fear

Al was admitted to the hospital emergency room and then to the inpatient unit for overnight observation. The diagnostic studies confirmed a small stroke. Nobody ever looks good in a hospital gown. I was shocked and scared, even more so to watch this brilliant man struggle to write his name. By morning, his condition had improved and he returned home, slowed for sure. I knew we were on a downward slope and feared that rest and medications would not be enough. We were given just three lines of "Discharge Planning" notes.

In three days, I scheduled a consultation with Al's cardiologist. The spare waiting room invited quiet, attentive demeanor, searching walls for anything to see or read.


## In the Waiting Room

Mapped in red and blue—
arteries, veins and muscle,
Eden's perfect heart.

His a noble heart
stented, healing, buying time,
hope, a miracle.

I will never forget being called in to the examining room and seeing Al sitting on the table – downcast and shirtless, electrodes wired across his chest. Despite triple by-pass surgery twenty years ago, his heart function had weakened and cardiac catheterization would be necessary. We reminded ourselves that his by-pass surgery had been a remarkable success; now, we needed to address this new problem. One month later, in June, a cardiac stent was installed. He seemed to regain his strength. We moved on with our lives, enjoying our usual interests. He finished his two-year term as president of our neighborhood association and I continued writing and exploring the possibilities of a book.

By early autumn, he was growing weaker and more fatigued. The cardiac team recommended a pacemaker in order to stabilize his heart function. In November, on Election Night, he was wheeled into surgery and a pacemaker was installed above his heart. I remember lying on the hospital bed with my sister while he was in the operating room. Election reports moved across the small TV screen mounted on a wall bracket at the end of the bed. I could not have cared less.


## Priorities

Election Day news,
interminable chatter
matter not at all.

Here in this small room
words are few, hope resting in
a skillful surgeon's hands.

Remember today's gift
of morning, noon and night…
yesterday's as well.

The surgeon's report, delivered at 2am, was positive: the pacemaker was installed and working. My sister and I returned to my car, tired yet hopeful. Would this little mechanical instrument, seemingly miraculous intervention, put us back on track to a normal life? We prayed our way home, thanking God, and asking for more.

After discharge, the pacemaker brought us a new monthly task of "interrogating" it over a land telephone. This entailed attaching electrodes to his hairy chest and plugging them into a small receiver box connected to the telephone. The pacemaker's internal clicking rode over the telephone wires to some distant technician who announced each stage of the process and directed me to hold a magnet over the pacemaker planted surgically just under Al's skin. This continued until the technician was satisfied that an adequate recording had been accomplished. We were in awe of this technology, Al, especially.


## Life Source

Breaths
come loudly
whirring
over morning's quiet
one after another,
layers of anima
stirring up from some fleshy tunnel
unraveling mysteries
along intimate pathways.

We approached Thanksgiving and Christmas with uneven energies and anxiety. Holiday decorations remained in storage and social activities were limited. We made a few medical appointments before being held hostage by heavy snows in January. Meanwhile, I noticed Al weakening again, but he insisted he was simply a little tired. I was learning more about these things and it became clear to me that he was having a stroke. His movements were slowed and his words garbled. He pulled me to him and uttered a broken "I'm so sorry." I called for an ambulance. He was rushed to the hospital emergency room where he was transformed into a patient and I into a terrified partner.


## Emergency Room

Curtains divide only space,
not desperate hope from sinking reality,
not private terror from public conversation,
not today's crisis from tomorrow's unknown.

Curtains swing free, riding on rings and rails.
Voices and feet move in on intimacy,
one side of the bed, then the other,
practiced, commanding trust.

Swallow fear.  Coil it down
into some dark place
out of sight
for now.

Al regained his strength and speech after just three days. He was discharged with instructions for medicines and a follow-up appointment with our family doctor. Within twenty-four hours, he was clearly disabled and we returned to the hospital. This time, he had suffered a major stroke, left side. It left him with right arm and right leg disability, a very damaged swallowing mechanism, and expressive aphasia, a condition which impairs the ability to speak or express oneself, even in the most ordinary ways. I wrote in my journal, "Cried all the way home …Al sobbed his heart out today and we sobbed with him. He is really crushed by this." (2/25/05)


## Between times

Is this what I shall remember—
glazed over grief
settling in
like sweaters folded,
not resisting,
waiting in boxes
until the days
grow short again?

Hospitalization lasted two weeks, then two months in rehabilitation. While we were both grieving, we also knew we would have to work hard to achieve recovery. He applied himself diligently to all therapies and won the affection and support of staff. I visited him daily to cheer him on, applaud staff, and advocate for him when necessary. Later, I wrote in my journal, "This is the end of my life as I've known it. I want a martini, Al's martini." (3/13/05)

62


## Applesauce Down

*"A spoonful of sugar*
*helps the medicine go down ..."* *

Small covered cups,
a spoon, a hand, lilting voices,
promises of health
and better things to come,
but one thing is certain:
*Applesauce never* again!


*"A Spoonful of Sugar" by Robert Sherman from Walt Disney Productions *Mary Poppins*

## Getting There …

Time to sob
scream
grip the wheel
fling grief to the doors
let it return like an echo
still throbbing.
Hold it close
comforted
by the telling

## …And Back

Light snow
sun now and then
little wind and rain
moon back again
easy commutes
kind deeds every day
others praying
Hope abides
in simple things.

Meanwhile, I began handling many lifestyle issues. All legal matters had to be resolved so that I could manage our financial issues and Al's health care. I began retrofitting our home to accommodate a wheelchair, provide adequate access to bedroom and bathroom, and assure overall safety and ease for him and for me as his caregiver. I wrote in my journal, "…the most painful part of all this is my shifting perspectives on this person I've known and loved for almost forty years…he has been assaulted in mind and heart…something so total, so personal. I don't want to say it aloud." (5/15/05)


## Losing Hold

Long days and nights
become weeks and months
of waiting, hoping, fearing to hope,
losing hold of life
as I know it,
hanging on
to remnants
of the familiar,
imagining
a new whole
less than
I had
had.

With Al enrolled in inpatient rehabilitation, I returned to an aborted writing project – a book to  help people in all walks of life keep brief records of their lives, day by day, whatever they want to remember, like the journal I had been keeping for two years. *My Life Matters: A Persoonal Record, One Day at a Time* was published in late 2005. (Al had been pivotal in choosing the title.) I sold nearly 100 copies in a few months, reassured by knowing I had another life apart from care giving, advocacy, and legal and personal challenges of the spousal caregiver.


## In the Window, Longing

Flakes
slow gathering
swirl across this gray afternoon
spin into air    disappear midway down
Oh, to catch one
sweet on my tongue,
be in-spired

Al's two months in rehabilitation resulted in his meeting critical discharge planning goals. He learned to walk with a cane and leg brace, get up and down short flights of stairs and maintain suitable balance to avoid falls, always with me or someone ready to lend a hand. He learned to handle basic tasks of daily living, usually with some level of acceptable assistance. His ability to communicate a simple thumb-up or thumb-down for "yes" or "no" improved, as did his overall alertness and involvement in activities. At some level, I was becoming more accepting. I wrote, "It pleases me to know one hundred seventy-five people are out there writing…I've made little money but I've made healthy strides in friendship and self-confidence." (MLM 12/31/05)


## Questions After Speech Therapy

What do we know of *words*
Ideas    images    tales and stories    letters and numbers
strung out on a page
the shape of things reflected in hidden places behind the eye?

What do we know of *speech*
sighs    cries    songs, sonnets and simple tunes    words tumbling
out across the tongue
the sounds of things rushing into the ear's own cavern?

What do we know of *memory*
moment to moment    the distant past    how to tie a shoe or write
a note
the recall of things    named    seen    heard    spoken    the stuff
of being one with others?

What do we know of *love*
feelings    hurt    pain    joy    tenderness remembered
the gift of a word or two    a touch    a smile    a wish already
known, unspoken?

Al's coming home meant a whole new way of life for us. While confined to a wheelchair, he was very motivated to practice walking and strengthening exercises. A stream of Medicare-approved home therapy sessions began on a weekly basis. I knew this was a good thing, but it also required more organizing tasks for me to schedule therapists and work with Al myself in order to make these gains secure. By Medicare protocols, these therapies ended after six weeks. I engaged a home aide for five hours a week to give me a break.

## Three Hands Under the Tap,

Warm water and splashing suds
slide over palms and fingers
and a new day.

## Stepping Out

He puts his good foot
down into the darkness,
his cane a wobbly companion,
and steals a glance at the night sky
clear, awash with stars
and streaking planes,
the moon brilliant
white and full.

He stops, rolls
his head back slowly,
lets it rest there,
exclaims at the splendor
spread out above him
and looks down again,
seeking his place
on an earthly path.

Al continued to improve in important ways, physically, intellectually, and socially. But walking, right arm movements, and speech were permanently impaired. He had been a published writer and avid reader, but seemed unable to do either. He had been a very social and ambitious person in virtually any area of endeavor, so continuing some semblance of our former lifestyle was important to both of us. Theater, restaurants, church activities, and family events continued to be sources of pleasure, though modified. And, I hoped, of moderate recovery.


## Making Progress

He has come a long way.
Does he know?
Does it matter?
He lifts one foot,
then the other,
intent on the task at hand,
no mere glancing about allowed.
Extraordinary will returns
like an old friend,
past victories lost to silence.

Destiny Mall announced their new Live at the Met Series. We decided to test access there for "I Puritani"—underground parking, elevator to the top, good seats with wheelchair spaces. Later, my essay, "Something Grand in the Theater" was published in our local newspaper. I told myself that such little "leaps" would keep me healthy and intact. Despite this and other small important victories, I could not always make it through the night without waking, restless and worried.


## Insomnia

Night's unremitting dark
settles down, spreads
through the house—
ambience for solitary talk,
a conversation inward.
Bright red numbers move
across the clock face,
blinking one after another,
like a finger wagging
inescapable truth

I began to see life as a series of unsettling events while trying to stay balanced and committed to enjoying a few more years together with some acceptable level of comfort. Slow drives in the country were a favorite pastime. He exclaimed vocally or pointed at passing sights—landscapes, houses, barns, buildings, and people. Some things he had seen before. I don't believe he had forgotten; rather, it didn't matter. They could be enjoyed again.

## A Rope of Clouds Rolls Across the Sky

twirled   frayed   black and gray
spilling hard driving rain
against the wipers chasing
silver linings
on the other side

Eight months later, unrelated and exploratory surgery due to a spot on Al's pancreas was scheduled, followed by five weeks in rehabilitation due to complications from the surgery. I never understood the outcomes from surgery and struggled with the possibility that something had happened to him in surgery, yet knowing well his overall set of disabilities. Rehabilitation was never really "rehabilitation;" his care in the nursing home was barely minimal. I visited him for hours every day, unable to change the course of his condition. It was becoming clear to me and visiting family and friends that his health was deteriorating. Al died during the night hours of December 20, 2007, alone, in his bed at the rehabilitation facility. The Immediate Cause" on the death certificate read "Complications of pancreatitis and pancreatic pseudocyst." I obsessed for days on his lonely death, how I could have been with him, would he have even known. I was counselled to move on, that I had done all I could do. We celebrated Al's life in the Roman Catholic Rite of Christian Burial, with his large family and many friends in attendance, several of whom participated in the readings and musical selections.

Through the two and one-half years of his stroke, modest recovery, and final illness, we enjoyed remarkable kindnesses from many people. I like to think of that as a "leavening agent" helping us move along into a whole new lifestyle in the earlier period of our story, then helping us through his final and devastating illness. I came to see that wishing for an end to the nightmare was foolhardy; the ability to see it through was the only path to choose. Taking a few short breaths now and then remained a powerful and therapeutic tool in getting beyond the hurdles. Reliance on the gift and hard work of writing, as laid down in this memoir, was also a therapeutic tool. Al and I had been blessed with nearly forty years of remarkable friendship and marriage which had nurtured us into the people were still becoming. Love was at the heart of that experience. I am confident in the telling and hopeful that it finds resonance with readers.


**To Care is to Heal**

the broken places, the pain.
Grateful heart receives,
love endures.

**Solo**


Quite unexpectedly, a box seat was mine tonight.
The Symphony was playing Brahms' Double Concerto

for Violin and Cello – soloists of renown, side by side,
strings and woodwinds musing on their conversation;

orchestral lines grand and nuanced, *allegro, andante,
vivace non troppo.*  Like life lived wisely.  Believe me.

You would have loved it!  But not my seat tonight.
I looked down to where we sat, sometimes hand in hand,

where wheel chairs are aligned.  Tonight, tears fell on stairs
you could not climb, on notes you could not hold.  And yet,

it seemed so clear that life goes on; this, too, a milestone,
one seat, a single ticket in hand.

## After Memoir, Almost

It is now late January and we are beyond the "holiday season." Here and there, outdoor  decorations reflect either reluctance to leave the holidays behind or just "not getting to it."  Some stores advertise items "on sale." Everywhere, nature reminds us of endings and the promise of beginnings, if we attend to its stewardship. Personally, this time of year evokes both nostalgia and an abiding sense of loss of those I have loved who have passed away, countered by a mindset focused on a healthy and grateful celebration of the season. I am not, by nature, an effective planner except in a short-range mindset. Life unfolds. I have only a modest impact on the outcome. Perhaps that is the key purpose of "memoir"—to mine the past for a sense of self, enough that the writer can leave it there, more deftly open to the stories and found truths that follow.

## Gift of Unknowing

Last night,
I lay on a patio lounge under a cloud
brushed canopy of stars, moon nearly full,
Jupiter in view, the passing aroma of lilac
overtaking sensibility and setting me free
to imagine myself into the sky, become
one with it, make it my own. From there,

it was an easy turn
to recall a favorite childhood escape
to our beloved old lilac in full bloom,
crawl under its twisted crusty branches
and imagine myself the center of things,
everyone and everything arranged for *me*,
the ruse continuing until I grew tired of it.

Resettling
into the patio lounge,
I tried to imagine the same scenario,
engage that sense of power and position,
of not knowing truth from fantasy.

I could only remember it.

# Homage to Hokusai: A Poet's Found Truth
*After The Great Wave Off Kanagawa*


Might Hokusai have imagined snow in the thrust
of the great wave billowing up and over itself,
rogue that it was, rushing ahead on a cresting sea,
Mt. Fugi silent, keeping watch?

No, it is I who search for the familiar, imagining
massive steel plows, their wings tossing snowdrifts,
salt and sand high and to the side, the roar of it all,
and in summer, their quiet waiting in tall grass,
their feats noted in municipal logs and tales
of epic winters battled and now reframed
in the lens of changing climate realities.

We, too, are creatures of the seasons, our lifetimes—
work and play, joy and woe, triumph and defeat,
roads taken, histories revealed.
It is all of a piece.
A time to rest and a time to push on,
to dare the billowing wave to carry us through
to a new season, new wisdom, always mindful
of artistic intention and a careful hand.


Note: Katsushika Hokusai, ukiyo-e artist of the Edo period was said to have moved ninety times in his lifetime. He was apprenticed to a wood-carver and was later trained in print design under famous Kabuki Theater designers. He began wandering through the country in 1793 and was said to have changed his artistic name twenty times. He is known historically as Hokusai, earning a living by selling his popular woodcuts and prints. *Thirty-Six Views of Mt. Fugi* was the most famous of his published books, and it continues to hold sacred significance in Japan and internationally. It is among its pages that one finds his iconic painting, *The Great Wave Off Kanagawa.* It was completed in 1831 and measures one foot three inches by ten inches. The USPS selected it for a postage stamp. It was on display at the Fine Arts Museum, Boston Massachusetts in 2023. Hokusai died in poverty in 1849.

## Last Conversation


I cannot stay away this morning.
Like the woodpecker
relentless among your hollow places,
the wren touching down on a low branch,
I am compelled to attend

to your last winter,
Old Friend.
Each day, more of your bark falls away
leaving naked harder stuff, the core
of what you have become.  So shall it be for me.

I capture you on film
straight on, still and alone,
or posed with other old friends—
the log shed you sheltered, the brook rushing by,
the fir tree and the elderly sycamore.  The wrens
will miss you in the spring, the fireflies in June.

I am with you 'til the end,
Old Friend,
as you are brought to earth, crashing
across the lawn and carried away in pieces,
leaving chips and yellow wood dust
like unsettled carpets

around your vast ringed base
where life lines, running full and slender, swirl
through knots and darker places—your time
here affirmed.  And at the outer edges, mine, too,
our silent presence to each other
by one of us remembered.

**Mary Gardner** traces her love for words and writing to winning a standard English-language dictionary in 4th grade and to three years of Latin and French in high school and college. Her poems have been honored internationally, regionally and locally by their inclusion in many anthologies and/or receiving awards through those venues. FootHills Publishing published her three chapbooks of poetry as a trilogy. She holds a Certificate in Poetry from the Downtown Writers Center, YMCA, Syracuse, NY which is affiliated with independent writing programs across the United States. In a previous career, she published twenty articles on human resources and management development and earned a Master of Public Health degree from Johns Hopkins University. She is an active member and former president of the CNY Branch, National League of American Pen Women. She enjoys, and is enriched by, the company of family and friends and various commitments with community groups.